SOUTH AFRIC
LAND OF SPLENDOUR

To Helen & Colin
Thanks for such wonderful hosts!
Love, Michael (

PLACE OF GOLD

Little more than a century ago the treasure-house of the Witwatersrand – the 'ridge of white waters' – looked over a bleak Highveld countryside. Today the region, now called Gauteng, functions as the fast-beating heart of South Africa's dynamic economy: much of it is occupied by two major cities and a dense conurbation of mining, and industrial towns which, together, accommodate a fifth of the population. By far the busiest of the centres is Johannesburg *(left)*, seat of the provincial

government and South Africa's financial capital – a city that was founded on gold and still retains something of the brash digger days about it, its rugged origins evident in the frantic pace of business and social life and in an almost universal preoccupation with money. It is also a city of striking contrasts – of wealth and poverty, of affluent tree-lined suburbs and dusty, overcrowded townships whose residents struggle for the basic decencies of life. Best-known is Soweto, home to two million people.

Johannesburg has much to offer the visitor. Here you'll find quality hotels, glittering malls, gourmet restaurants, an exuberant nightlife, and a lively performing arts scene that embraces some of the most exciting music to have emerged from Africa. And, although the metropolis has few claims to beauty – its highrise central area is almost devoid of greenery – the surrounding suburbs boast some lovely parks and gardens.

So, too, does Pretoria, a little over 50 km to the north and known as the Jacaranda City for the exquisite, lilac-flowered trees that bring springtime glory to its thoroughfares *(above left)*. Pretoria is South Africa's administrative capital, its corridors of power enclosed within the elegant, crescent-shaped Union Buildings *(above)*. Some of the imposing statuary in the latter's meticulously maintained grounds evokes the spirit of an earlier, rather more militaristic era.

PALACE OF PLEASURE

Rising grandly and somewhat incongruously from the sunburnt bushveld, a two hour drive to the north-east of Johannesburg, is an ornately domed and decorated edifice that, in the words of hospitality tycoon Sol Kersner, is 'a fantasy come to life'. This is the Palace of the Lost City, rated among the world's most unusually conceived, and most lavish, inland resorts.

The Palace, evoking images of a past that never really was – of Ophir and Sheba and fabulous kingdoms hidden away in the jungle depths – is the latest addition to the Sun City hotel, casino and leisure complex. No expense has been spared in its construction, ornamentation and operation: the entrance foyer rises cathedral-like to its lofty, painted ceiling *(opposite page, right)*; a life-sized model of Shawu *(left)* guards the mosaic-tiled courtyard leading

off the Elephant Walk; sumptuous restaurants, state-of-the-art suites and superlative service cosset the clientele in luxurious comfort.

In the grounds are inviting walkways, waterways and pools (one of which is large enough to have its own beach and artificially contrived surfing waves), an Arizona-style golf course, and a magnificent, 3 500-tree forest that incorporates species drawn from around the world.

The older established parts of the Sun City resort have much to offer the visitor, including three fine hotels that cater for all tastes; glittering gaming rooms, cordon bleu eateries, nightspots, theatres, cinemas, a Superbowl that serves as a venue for top international shows and sporting spectaculars, and some of the country's most beautifully landscaped gardens. Among the outdoor features are a 750-metre long, man-made lake, and a golf course that hosts the world's top players.

A PEOPLE AND THEIR ART

The rural South Ndebele people, many of whom live in the region to the north of Pretoria, are renowned for their brightly coloured murals and their elaborate style of dress.

Traditionally, the walls of Ndebele homesteads – rectangular dwellings surrounded by courtyards – were painted in simple, bold patterns of triangles, chevrons and squares, but with greater exposure to urban ways (and with the availability of synthetic paints) the range of colours and designs has expanded to include recognizable subjects such as animals, birds and city scenes.

The murals are created by the women of the family, who are themselves almost works of art when adorned in their bright blankets, beaded aprons and metal ornamentation. The rings or *dzilla* that encircle their ankles, arms and necks are more or less permanent fixtures.

SCENIC WONDERLAND

For sheer visual splendour few parts of southern Africa can compare with the Eastern Transvaal's Escarpment, a range of grand mountains and deep valleys that runs some 300 km northwards from the provincial capital of Nelspruit. The region's most prominent physical feature is the Blyde River Canyon *(right)*, a massively majestic gorge whose cliff faces fall steeply, in places precipitously, for almost a kilometre to the river below. Among other attractive elements in the area is the village of Pilgrim's Rest *(top)*, born in the heady days of an early gold rush and now preserved in its charming entirety as a 'living museum'.

SOUTH AFRICA'S EDEN

The heat-hazed Lowveld plain, below and to the east of the Escarpment, is big-game country, much of it occupied by the famed Kruger National Park, some by a half-dozen or so splendid private reserves. The Kruger is sanctuary for more varieties of wildlife than any other major reserve in Africa, its 137 mammal species embracing the 'big five' of the animal kingdom – lion *(above)*, leopard, elephant, buffalo and rhino – as well as the endangered wild dog *(left)*, the spotted hyaena *(right)* and a myriad impala *(above right)*. Overnight visitors are accommodated in the 20 or so pleasant, tree-shaded rest camps, like this one at Shingwedzi *(top left)*.

SOME PLAY, SOME PREY

The Kruger is also home to about 500 different kinds of bird, including these whitebacked vultures *(right)* and a superb array of other raptors. But the park's most prominent residents are its larger creatures – the great predators, the crocodiles and hippos of the luxuriant riverine reaches, the giraffe, the wildebeest, the kudu, roan, waterbuck, sable and other antelope. Among the herbivores are more than 30 000 Burchell's zebra *(above left)*, found throughout the region.

Biggest of the animals are the elephants *(above right)*, of which there are about 8 000. These giants of the veld are gentle enough if unmolested: they have no natural enemies (except man), and they flourish in the Kruger. But they are voracious feeders – an adult male gets through 300 kg of vegetation in a day – and they can inflict heavy damage on the environment if their numbers aren't strictly controlled.

SAFARI IN STYLE

Sprawling along the Kruger's western boundary are some of the world's largest privately owned wildlife reserves – and most sophisticated game lodges. For decades fences separated them from the next-door national park, but these have now been removed and the animals roam freely over the wider area. Guests are exceptionally well looked after, pampered even, sleeping in spacious, often luxuriously appointed chalets, enjoying five-star cuisine and service, exploring the game-filled bushveld in custom-built safari vehicles in the company of rangers who are both personable and intimately versed in the ways of the wild.

NIGHT EYES

For those who spend their bush holiday at a private safari lodge, a notable feature of camp life is the night drive – an escorted excursion into the darkness aboard a four-wheel-drive equipped with spotlights. The game-viewing is often as rewarding as that during the day since lion *(top left)* and many other predators hunt under cover of darkness and smaller creatures like the large-spotted genet *(right)*, bushbabies, and civet are nocturnal by habit.

Other evenings are enjoyed in the firelit *boma*, the open-air enclosure where one gathers for the evening meal. This is invariably a sumptuous affair in which barbecued venison features prominently and where, with the stars above and the night time sounds of the bush all around, the talk is animated, dwelling on the day's sightings and of the moods and mysteries of the wild kingdom.

GOLDEN GATEWAY

For the most part the Free State countryside is flattish, windswept, devoid of trees, visually monotonous, but towards the east the land rises in a series of dramatically weathered sandstone hills, their colours (imparted by iron oxides) ranging from reddish through deep orange to golden brown to create strikingly eye-catching landscapes. Two of the formations – twin 100-metre high buttresses that stand like massive gateway sentinels – have given their name to the Golden Gate National Park, a 12 000-hectare expanse of ridges and ramparts lying in the valley of the Little Caledon River. Visitors are drawn to the park mainly for its scenic splendour, though it also has its wildlife, including wildebeest and zebra, grey rhebok, mountain reedbuck, stately eland and shy oribi. Elsewhere in the eastern Free State there are fields of cosmos in autumn *(above right)* and fertile farmlands that yield rich harvests of maize and wheat, golden sunflowers, cherries, peaches and other fruits.

VALLEY OF DESOLATION

Covering nearly half a million square kilometres of the South African interior are the immense, lonely plains of the Great Karoo, an enormous semi-wilderness of sandy soils and sparse vegetation, low rainfall and clear, bone-dry air. There is good underground water, though, which is tapped by a myriad windmills *(right)* scattered across the vast sheep farms of the region. Most of the Karoo's terrain is flat, but here and there ancient volcanic action has created ridges and sills ('kopjes', or rocky outcrops) that, over the aeons have been weathered by wind and periodic flood into strikingly stark formations. The most spectacular of these is perhaps the Valley of Desolation *(above)*, a towering jumble of craggy heights overlooking the historic town of Graaff-Reinet in the south-east.

BARRIER OF SPEARS

The awesome rampart of mountains known as the Drakensberg, the most dramatic segment of the Great Escarpment that fringes South Africa's U-shaped perimeter, runs along KwaZulu-Natal's border with the kingdom of Lesotho. Its eastern face falls virtually sheer for 2 000 metres and more to the foothills, and these, in turn, give way to the coastal plain that gently rolls away to the Indian Ocean.

The massifs and peaks have descriptive names – the Sentinel, the Organ Pipes, Devil's Tooth, the Amphitheatre, Champagne Castle, the Mitre, the Chessmen, Monk's Cowl, Mushroom Rock and so on. Among the prominent formations is

the Mont-aux-Sources ('mountain of springs') complex, so called for the number of rivers that rise on its plateau-like summit. Among these are the Elands, which runs away northwards to join the Vaal, and the Tugela. The latter plunges over the rim of the Amphitheatre in a spectacular, 850-metre long series of cascades and cataracts *(left)*, one of which is the country's highest waterfall. The Tugela's course leads through and beyond the Royal Natal National Park, a scenically enchanting upland sanctuary for the fascinating flora of the area, for antelope and other mammals, and for 200 species of bird, including a splendid parade of raptors. One of these is the bearded vulture *(far left)* found only in upper reaches of mountains in the Drakensberg and Lesotho. Of special interest – here and among the hills to the south – are the ancient Bushman paintings *(previous page)* that decorate the cliff faces and the walls of numerous caves.

COASTAL WONDERLAND

Nudging Zululand's Indian Ocean coast is the Greater St Lucia Wetland Park, a huge, beautiful and remarkably diverse marine and wetland complex of lagoon, marshland, savanna, forest, high dune, pristine shoreline, ocean and the world's most southerly off-shore coral reefs. Central feature of the park is its shallow, 36 000-hectare 'lake' (in reality an extensive estuarine system), home to crocodile and hippo and to flocks of pelicans, flamingos and other aquatic birds. The lake and its surrounds are a paradise for hikers, naturalists, fishermen *(left)*, boating enthusiasts, and game viewers. Part of the wetland park is occupied by the Mkuzi Reserve, among whose residents are white rhino *(above left)*.

ENDLESS SAFARI

Northern KwaZulu-Natal is famed for its wildlife: a warm climate, high rainfall (in normal years) and the consequent luxuriance of plant life combine to provide superb habitats for a remarkable profusion of animals and birds. Foremost among the region's half-dozen or so major game reseves is the Hluhluwe-Umfolozi park, a pioneer in rhino conservation and a magnificent expanse of wooded hill, floodplain and riverine forest. Each of the other conservancies, though, has its own distinctions and its beauty. For visitors, there are walking trails, bird hides, game-viewing roads *(above)*, comfortable rest camps and secluded bush lodges *(left)*.

WARRIORS AND DRUMBEATS

The Zulu nation is relatively young: it was founded, by the great warrior-king Shaka, only in the early 1800s. Prior to his succession to the chieftainship the clan, just one of about 800 groups of the Eastern Nguni, numbered an insignificant 1 500 members, but by introducing new weapons (notably the short stabbing-spear and longer body-length shield), new battle tactics and through brilliant leadership, he led his fearless and well-disciplined warriors to victory after victory, and within a few years was in control of the country's entire eastern seaboard.

Eventually (in 1879), British guns and regimental discipline broke the military power of the Zulu – but not the pride of the people. Their culture remains largely intact, a splendid heritage that is at its most visible in the remoter rural areas and in the various 'living museums' of the region where traditional crafts, ceremonies and dancing can be viewed. Dress styles vary from clan to clan, though most incorporate intricate beadwork; hides, pelts, plumes and ox-hide shields are a feature of pulsating displays of Zulu music and dance. The range of Zulu handcrafts includes sturdy clay pottery *(above)*; notable, too, is the basketware and wooden carvings. A prominent element in Zulu traditional religious belief and ceremonies is the *sangoma* – a spirit medium and diviner *(right)*.

TAKING TO THE SEA

Durban is South Africa's third city and premier seaport, its high maritime status underpinned by one of the southern hemisphere's most splendid natural harbours. It is also a popular holiday playground of sun, sea, surf, sand and a sophisticated array of entertainment venues. Most tourist attractions are concentrated along what is known as the Golden Mile, a six-kilometre city seafront that boasts broad beaches, piers, pools and pavilions, elegant hotels, nightspots, restaurants and glittering shopping malls. Among its more colourful features are the elaborately decorated rickshas *(above right)* that ply the promenade route, and a small-craft harbour full of bobbing yachts *(right)*.

Other drawcards include the tropical Indian Ocean fish and performing seals and dolphins of Sea World, the reptiles of the Fitzsimons Snake Park, the scale-model city of Minitown, and the Amphitheatre, an enchanting beachside sunken garden of flowers, lawns and summer houses.

Although Durban is KwaZulu-Natal's largest urban centre, it is not the provincial capital. That status belongs to Pietermaritzburg, set among the misty green hills some 90 km inland and an elegant place of red-brick Victorian buildings (the City Hall, *right*, is perhaps the most notable) and gardens bright with roses and azaleas. Among its more eye-catching edifices is the pagoda-style pavilion that graces Alexandra Park *(above right)*.

LAND OF THE XHOSA

Perhaps the most distinctive natural feature along the famed Wild Coast is the Hole-in-the-Wall *(above)*, a massive detached cliff whose arched opening receives a thundrous surge of surf (indeed the rock is known to the locals as *esiKhaleni*, which means 'place of noise'). The coast and its hinterland of rolling hills, forested valleys and a myriad perennial rivers and streams are the historic home of the Xhosa people, a group embracing a multiplicity of clans, dialects and cultures.

SETTLER COUNTRY

Port Elizabeth, a city whose attractions include some charming old terraced houses facing Donkin Street *(above right)* and a world-class oceanarium renowned for its performing dolphins *(right)*, owes its origins to a colonial scheme to 'pacify' the troubled frontier region of the 1820s. The surrounding 'settler' country has much to offer visitors, not least the Addo Elephant National Park *(above)*, a rugged expanse of bush terrain that serves as sanctuary for the remnants of the Eastern Cape's once-great herds of elephant and buffalo.

GARDEN ROUTE

Two hundred years ago a celebrated French visitor grew lyrical in his praise of one particular stretch of the southern seaboard – Nature, he said, had made 'an enchanted abode' of the coastal region we now know as the Garden Route. And, in essence, little has changed over the centuries. The shoreline is still a magical compound of capes and cliffs, lagoons and lakes, lovely forest-flanked rivers and estuaries *(above)*, golden beaches and secluded bays. Inland the mountains – the Tsitsikamma, the Outeniqua, the Langeberg – rise in wooded splendour, their slopes cut through by scores of tumbling perennial streams. And in between is the coastal terrace, the 'garden' that, although now built up in places, retains its luxuriant beauty. It also has its wildlife

species, among them the Cape clawless otter *(previous page)* which lives in and around the rivers. Foremost among the region's resort towns are Plettenberg Bay, whose beach area is dominated by Beacon Island and its hotel *(previous page)* and Knysna, linked to the largish centre of George by the Outeniqua Choo-Tjoe, a charming old Class 24 steam train *(above)* seen here crossing the Kaaiman's River mouth.

Farther inland, cradled between two high mountain ranges, is the Little Karoo, home of the ostrich farming industry that was born in the fashion-led feather boom of the 1890s and is still flourishing today *(right)*. Largest of the Little Karoo's towns is Oudtshoorn, north of which lie the Cango Caves *(above right)*, an extensive series of labyrinthine caverns rated among the country's more remarkable natural wonders.

TAVERN OF THE SEAS

Cape Town is the oldest and arguably the most attractive of South Africa's cities, its central area set snugly between the massive, flat-topped bulk of Table Mountain on one side and historic Table Bay on the other. The mountain, rising more than 1 000 metres above sea level, ranks among the world's best-known landmarks, drawing half a million and more visitors to its summit each year. Most make their way up by cable-car *(above right)*, a five-minute trip during which breathtaking vistas unfold. The views from the top are even grander in their scope.

Rivalling Table Mountain as a tourist drawcard are the city's sunlit beaches, its time-honoured buildings, its museums, galleries and myriad

cosmopolitan restaurants, its lively calendar of arts – among other things, the mixed-descent community has charming musical traditions *(right)* – and, above all, its new and marvellously animated Victoria & Alfred Waterfront. This last is a place full of festival and delight; among its enticements are speciality shops by the hundred, eateries, bistros, pubs, cinemas (including the giant Imax), theatres, a maritime museum, an oceanarium, open quaysides, promenades and bustling public squares.

AMONG THE VINES

The Cape Peninsula extends southwards from the city, a slender, 75-km long promontory that comprises, for the most part, a strikingly beautiful mountain range that is at its loftiest in the heights of Table Mountain itself. Among the most pleasant of day-excursions is the round-the-Peninsula coastal route, one of whose stretches takes you over the high and scenically stunning Chapman's Peak Drive *(above left)* between the harbour town of Hout Bay and the quiet village of Noordhoek. Worthwhile inland digressions lead you to the famed Kirstenbosch Botanical Garden *(left)*, where about half the country's 18 000 species of flowering plant are nurtured and to Groot Constantia *(above right)*. The latter is the oldest and stateliest of the region's Cape Dutch homesteads and centrepiece of an estate that has been producing fine wines for centuries.

WHERE TWO OCEANS MEET

The Peninsula ends in a high headland known as Cape Point – not quite the southernmost extremity of Africa but near enough, and famed for the magnificent views the summit commands. The Point, commonly held to be the meeting place of the Atlantic and Indian oceans, is part of the Cape of Good Hope Nature Reserve, a 7 750-hectare sanctuary that sustains the region's unique *fynbos* ('fine bush') flora. In springtime, when the wild flowers bloom, the countryside is a riot of colour. The reserve's 40-km coastline is much favoured by fishermen, snorklers and scuba-divers *(right)*.

UNDER THE OAKS

The centuries have treated Stellenbosch kindly. The town, set in the lovely valley of the Eerste ('first') River north-east of Cape Town, was born in 1679 and grew up with grace, its thatched and limewashed houses, historic public buildings and its avenues shaded beneath canopies of stately oak trees. Cultivating grapes and making wine have been the area's principal pre-occupations since the earliest days, and the surrounding hillsides and valleys are mantled by time-honoured vineyards.

HARBOURS AND HAMLETS

The country's western seaboard is a dry, sparsely populated, rather bleak region, its northern and more section known as Namaqualand. But it has its attractions and in places, its beauty. A flourishing fishin industry sustains a number of charming little coastal villages, the largest of which is Lambert's Bay *(above right)*, known for its seabird colonies on Bird Island, home to huge numbers of Cape gannets, gulls and cormorants. It is in springtime, though, that the West Coast and its hinterland beckon: after the winter rains, when the seemingly barren land is gloriously covered by great carpets of wild flowers.

WHALE WATCH

The southernmost tip of the African continent is Cape Agulhas, which is the Portuguese word for needles – a name coined by early seafarers because they found that their compasses were unaffected by magnetic deviation but instead bore true north. The cape itself is undistinguished, a low headland that slips quietly into the ocean. But it has its lighthouse *(above)*, and inside a museum.

Hermanus, on the shores of Walker Bay farther along the coast towards Cape Town, is notable for its Old Harbour – once a thriving centre of the fishing industry and now preserved as a museum – and for the bay's giant southern right whales. These great marine mammals make their way into the inshore waters each winter and spring to mate and give birth to their calves (the gestation period is a year), their arrival heralded by the town's 'whale crier' *(right)*.